Christine Clifford

Illustrations by Jack Lindstrom

University of Minnesota Press
Minneapolis London

Copyright 1998 by Christine Clifford

All rights reserved. No part of this publication may be reproduced, stored in a retrieval system, or transmitted, in any form or by any means, electronic, mechanical, photocopying, recording, or otherwise, without the prior written permission of the publisher.

Published by the University of Minnesota Press
111 Third Avenue South, Suite 290
Minneapolis, MN 55401-2520
http://www.upress.umn.edu

A Cataloging-in-Publication record for this book is available from the Library of Congress

ISBN 978-0-8166-4186-4 (PB)

Printed in the United States of America on acid-free paper

The University of Minnesota is an equal-opportunity educator and employer

20 19 18 17 16 15 14 13   10 9 8 7 6 5

A NOTE FROM THE AUTHOR TO CHILDREN

This book was written to help you explore the world of cancer with your family. Take this time to learn about the disease and ask all the questions you can.

It's important to talk about the feelings you may be having: fear and sadness, confusion or anger. Cancer isn't fair.

But through it all, know that you are loved and that you are special. You can help your family get through this experience because you bring a special piece to the puzzle: You.

This book is based on my family's experience. I hope that it helps you as you talk with your family. Thank you for using this book, and remember: Don't forget to laugh!

A NOTE FROM THE AUTHOR TO PARENTS

I was fifteen years old when my mother was diagnosed with breast cancer at age thirty-eight. The four children in our family watched in horror as our mother sank into a deep clinical depression. She stopped caring for her personal hygiene; she stopped communicating with us as children.

In those days we weren't even allowed to say the word "cancer." It was referred to as my mother's "illness" or "the C-word." We lived in fear that every day would be my mother's last day, and it had a profound effect on all of our lives.

My mother lived for four years after her diagnosis. I now realize what a tragedy and waste it was that we didn't embrace those four extra years of her life—to live each day as if it were one full life. So when I was diagnosed with the same cancer at the age of forty, I decided that in my family we would not waste any of the time that we had together.

I have written this book with the hope that *Our Family Has Cancer, Too!* will encourage you and your family to talk about the disease: to cry, to laugh, to learn, to explore, to fear, to care, but most of all, to live. Cancer can and will have a profound effect on every person in your family. But it's up to all of us—the patients, survivors, family, friends, caregivers, and employers—to help cancer patients and especially the children whose lives will be touched by this disease find a way to go on living, laughing, playing, and enjoying life.

Use this book as an opportunity for you to gather your family in a healthy, family-oriented discussion. Use it as a time to explore the possibilities of treatment, the changes that will take place, and the length of time it is going to take to get through a cancer experience. Encourage your children to ask their questions, and then take the time to research the answers.

> *The parents' notes sprinkled throughout will help you and your family start your discussions. You'll see them set off in a box like this.*

My family and I have lived fully for the two years since I was diagnosed with cancer. I feel proud that our family hasn't wasted one extra minute waiting for something else to happen. I wish you and your family the very best as you live together with your family's cancer experience.

And, by the way, don't forget to laugh! Real laughter always helps everyone to live and to love better—and that's what really counts.

DEDICATION

This book is dedicated to my family for their undivided love, support, understanding, and sense of humor.
My husband, John, and my two sons, Tim and Brooks, helped me turn an unhappy situation into a celebration of life.

Hi. My name is Tim. I'm a sixth grader at Valley View Middle School in Minnesota. I study pretty hard—math and science are my favorite subjects. I'm a green-belt in karate, I play baseball and soccer in the summer, and in the winter I like to ski and snow-board. I'm working toward my tenderfoot rank in Boy Scouts. Oh, yeah, I also take piano lessons.

I've lived in Minnesota all my life, and in case you haven't heard—it gets real cold here in the winter.

My younger brother, Brooks, is in the third grade. He plays hockey, baseball, and Sega, trades Star Trek and Magic cards, and tries to stay out of trouble, which isn't easy. Most of the time we get along—unless we're fighting over whose night it is to sleep with our dog.

By the way, our dog is a tricolored cocker spaniel named Sneakers. We named him that because he has white feet and a black and brown coat. My dad is a salesman, and my mom works as a marketing executive. We live in a cool neighborhood with tons of kids.

We all led a pretty normal life until one day . . . my mom and dad shared some important news.

They told us that my mom had cancer!

Have you ever heard of the word "cancer?" Cancer can be a scary word. Just the mention of the word makes my grandma and grandpa cry. They call it "the C-word" because they don't even like to say it.

I guess I had an idea of what cancer was. I knew it could make people really sick. Brooks knew a girl in the second grade who had a brain tumor. And one of our grandmothers died from cancer, too, before Brooks and I were even born.

I didn't know that cancer would become a big part of our lives.

> *You may wish to stop now and ask your children what they know about the word "cancer." Allow them to describe their reaction to the word. Then give them some information.*

The day we got the news—the day after Christmas, in fact—my mom and dad called a "family meeting." Brooks thought we were in trouble, and wondered if one of our pets had escaped again. I wasn't too worried, but I could tell by looking at Mom and Dad that they were concerned about something.

"Aren't we a lucky family?" Dad started out by asking us.

"Yes, we are," Brooks and I answered.

"Didn't we have a nice Christmas?" Dad questioned as he looked around at all the toys.

"We sure did," I said, while Brooks nodded his head in agreement.

"Well, sometimes along with the good things, some bad things happen to good people," Dad continued.

That's when Dad told us Mom had the disease called "cancer."

Brooks and I weren't totally sure what that meant. Dad explained that Mom was very sick. She looked the same to me and Brooks, but she was crying which made me feel sad. Dad said she had a lump called a "tumor." Mom's tumor was in her breast, but Dad explained that tumors can grow anywhere in the body. Mom said she would be going to the hospital to have some surgery that week. The operation would take out the cancer. Mom said she would only be in the hospital for a day or two.

"Can we come to the hospital, too?" Brooks asked.

Dad said we could come to visit, and Mom gave us both a big hug.

"Is it going to hurt, Mom?" Brooks asked, squeezing Sneakers even harder.

Mom said, "I probably will be very sore and tired after the operation. I'm going to need you both to be very brave."

"What if the operation doesn't get all the cancer?" I asked, moving closer to Mom.

Dad told us that just to be sure, Mom was going to have some other treatments, too. One was called "chemotherapy" and the other one was "radiation."

Dad told us chemotherapy would make Mom feel sick, and that she would probably lose her hair.

"Cool," I said, not even thinking, "now you'll look like Captain Picard on 'Star Trek'!" Mom and Dad laughed, and I felt good that they thought it was funny.

Brooks asked Dad why Mom was going to get sick. Dad explained that chemotherapy is a very powerful drug that's going to kill all the cancer cells. Because the drugs are so strong, he told us, sometimes some of the healthy cells are killed off, too. That's why Mom's hair would probably fall out.

We didn't like the "getting sick" part, but we didn't care about Mom's hair. We love her no matter what she looks like!

After we all finished talking, Brooks and I went back to playing with Sneakers and our new toys. But that night, when Mom was tucking me into bed, I asked her if she was going to die.

She gave me a big hug and told me she wasn't ready to leave this earth! "I'm going to fight this cancer with all my might," she said. "You and Brooks and Dad are going to help me win." And she said I should be sure to ask her any questions I had—because we were all in this together. I felt better, and I think she did, too.

I told Mom I loved her, and she said she loved me, too. When she left my room, I wasn't quite so scared.

This would be a good time to talk about your family's situation. Share your feelings with each other and your questions.

The next day, Mom took Brooks and me out to lunch at the Malt Shoppe for our favorite: cheeseburgers and strawberry malts. She told us more about the operation she was going to have, and said there would be lots of tubes, needles, and doctors.

We asked a lot of questions like "Who will stay with us while you're in the hospital?" and "Will we still be able to go on our family trip over spring vacation?"

"Either Gram or Dad will be home with you when I'm in the hospital," Mom replied. "And we'll have to see how I'm feeling before we plan any vacations."

Brooks asked Mom if cancer was contagious. She said it wasn't but that she needed to be extra careful not to catch colds or the flu from other people. She needed all her strength to fight the cancer.

After lunch, Mom took us shopping for some new tennis shoes, and we stopped to play some video games at the arcade.

When we were driving home, Mom said, "When I start my treatments I may not be able to do all the things we like to do, like go out for lunch. We'll just have to see how things go."

She told us we were going to need to be especially good, and that we might have to help around the house a little more in the days ahead.

> *Ask the children how they think they can help. Offer them some suggestions.*

THINK OF SOME WAYS YOU CAN HELP OUT A LITTLE MORE IN YOUR FAMILY

Some extra things I can do to help out:

_____

_____

_____

_____

_____

_____

_____

_____

_____

_____

That night, Brooks and Dad and I talked. We knew Mom was sad that she had cancer because we saw her crying. Suddenly Dad started crying and then Brooks started crying, too. Everyone was so sad that Mom said we should have a "crying party" to get it all out of our systems!

Mom and Dad told us it was OK to be sad or scared or angry, because they were, too. But if we all stuck together, along with the rest of our family and our friends, we would learn a lot about love and life in the months to come.

Already Mom was starting to forget things—like our piano lessons that afternoon. Brooks and I made a promise to give Mom lots of hugs and to be sure to tell her how much we love her.

Hey, it didn't just make Mom feel better, it made us feel better, too!

THE NEXT DAY
MOM WENT
TO THE
HOSPITAL
FOR HER
OPERATION.

Mom was in the hospital for three days. We visited her every day after school, and she was really glad to see us! She said she was sore, but the doctors gave her some pills to make her feel better.

We got to sit on her bed and watch a TV that was hung way up by the ceiling! Lots of people came to visit, including Gram and Grandpa, our Aunt Pam from New York, and friends of Mom's.

One night I got to eat the ice cream on her dinner tray. Brooks got to buy a candy bar from the vending machine. We missed having Mom home cooking our dinner, but we knew she needed to rest after the operation.

The day Mom got to come home from the hospital, we went with Dad to help her. There were lots of flowers to carry plus her suitcase, and we almost couldn't fit ourselves in the car!

A nurse wheeled Mom down to the front door of the hospital in a wheelchair. They told us that this was "hospital procedure."

Once Mom got home from the hospital, it was like a strange holiday. We had lots of visitors. The phone rang all the time, and the delivery man brought flowers several times a day. The flowers came in baskets, boxes, and vases, and we started putting some in every room in the house to cheer up my mom.

People started bringing over food, like lasagna and chicken casseroles. For a long time, Mom or Dad didn't even have to cook! Brooks and I didn't always like everything to eat, but Mom said we should be very grateful and always made us try the food. Of course, we always ate dessert, especially the carrot cake!

Mom explained that people were starting to hear the news about her cancer. She said it was OK to tell people what had happened to her because our good friends wanted to show their support. Other people who knew our family wanted us to know they cared about us, too.

Brooks said he shared the news of Mom's cancer with his class during "show and tell." All the kids in his class made Mom a huge get-well card. Brooks learned that there were lots of kids in his class who knew about cancer. Tommy's grandfather had prostate cancer five years ago. Allison's Aunt Kathy had lung cancer. Kelsey's Dad had cancer, too. Brooks was glad he had shared our news with his friends.

> *Discuss with your children who they can and cannot tell about your family's situation. You may choose to not tell certain people, or you may encourage them to share the news with whomever they wish. This is a good opportunity to talk about privacy issues—it's important to respect family privacy.*

A few weeks after Mom's operation, she started her chemo-therapy. We went with her to the oncology office one time to see what it was like.

The nurse took samples of Mom's blood from her arm. I've done that at the doctor before! Then she got hooked up to a thing called an "IV" that gave her the dose of drugs to kill the cancer.

We met some really neat people who were also cancer patients. One lady was a schoolteacher for the third grade—same as Brooks' teacher. She had skin cancer. There was a boy about my age who had cancer, too. His cancer was called leukemia, and he said it was a cancer of the blood. He and I got to play "Crazy Eights" with some cards while he had his treatment.

The cancer patients and visitors could watch TV, listen to the radio, or just sleep if they wanted to! The nurses gave me and Brooks some sugar cookies and told us we were welcome any-time.

Mom's hair did fall out, slowly at first, but then it fell out in big clumps. She started wearing wigs and hats. Brooks let her use some of his team baseball caps from his prized collection.

Once she even let our friends see her with no hair at all!

After several months of chemotherapy, Mom was ready to start "radiation" treatments. Dad explained that radiation was high-intensity rays, like from the sun or an x-ray machine, that would burn any cancer cells that were left.

When Mom started radiation treatment, the doctors marked her body with big, black Xs where the cancer had been so they could find the right spot to radiate each time. She let us come with her to see the radiation, too.

We saw the big machine that helped get rid of Mom's cancer cells. It looked like a giant space ship, and we got to talk to Mom through a monitor. We had to watch her treatment from a special room where we could be safe from the radiation rays since they were so strong.

Mom had to go to radiation every day for thirty-three days. Brooks and I made a batch of our special recipe chocolate-chip cookies and brought them to the doctors and nurses who were helping our Mom get better. They were sure glad to see us!

Our friends started getting curious about Mom being bald. Mike down the street said she looked like Uncle Fester! One of my friends said her head looked like a baseball and asked if he could autograph it!

Mom tried to keep up her spirits about losing her hair, but sometimes she was sad about it, too. Mom always said that the good news was that one day, after her treatments were over, her hair would grow back!

All of Mom's treatments made her real tired. She started taking naps every day, and sometimes she didn't have enough energy to do the things she used to do. It reminded me a lot of Grandpa. He naps every day, too!

Sometimes it didn't seem fair. We missed having Mom get up with us every morning to see us off to school. She didn't cook very much anymore, and she couldn't come to all of our school activities, like the school carnival or Pride Day.

But Brooks and I tried to be patient when Mom couldn't help us with our homework or come to all of our baseball games. We knew it was important for Mom's recovery for her to get lots of rest.

We helped around the house by answering the phone and watering the flowers Mom got. Sometimes we put signs on our front door that said, "Quiet! Mom is sleeping!"

Mom's cancer treatments lasted almost a whole year.

As the months passed by, Brooks and I did things to cheer Mom up. We baked brownies with sprinkles, made special cards, and picked flowers for her from our garden. In the winter we shoveled the snow so Mom could get out the driveway to her doctor appointments. We helped around the house by picking up our toys and making sure Sneakers had water in his dish.

Sometimes we bought her presents just to make her laugh! Brooks and I bought a funny hat with rabbit ears that said, "NO HARE DAY!"

We had a new routine around our house. It wasn't the same as before my mom got cancer, but our family found a way to deal with the changes cancer brought to our house.

Sometimes we made jokes about cancer, and sometimes we talked about how much we hated it. Sometimes we still cried, or still got scared.

We always made sure we talked about how we were feeling.

> *Create a schedule for your family to talk about the changes that are taking place. Evaluate how the changes have affected everyone's life, and let everyone share their feelings.*

One day my mom told us she was having her very last chemo treatment.

"We're all going out to celebrate!" she exclaimed.

"Are you all better, Mom?" asked Brooks, looking her up and down.

Mom explained that her cancer was now in "remission." This meant that she was healthy again, and she didn't have to have any more treatments.

That day the nurses gave Mom a cake, a certificate, and a pin that said "survivor." Dad took us all out for dinner, and Mom was laughing and smiling all night long.

"GOOD LUCK, MRS. CLIFFORD...WE'LL MISS YOU."

We learned a lot of new things during Mom's cancer treatment. We made some new friends, and we learned that there are people of all ages with cancer—both adults and kids. It was neat to exchange stories about what was happening with other kids dealing with cancer.

Jeff, a kid in my karate class, said his mom had cancer, too. They would sit around the dinner table and ask who had the most hair—his bald dad, his bald grandfather, or his mom, who was having chemotherapy.

We learned how we can be a better family with lots of love, support, and understanding. It was a difficult and scary experience, but now my mom says that we did it together—as a family. We helped to make my mom get better! But even if she hadn't gotten better, we shared lots of love, and had happy times when she was sick—and that's real important!

So if cancer comes to your house, to one of your parents, grand-parents, aunts, uncles, cousins, or even a brother or sister, don't be afraid. Talk about it with your family. Learn as much as you can. It helps everyone if you can keep your spirits up. Maybe you can even try to make everyone laugh as well as cry! Give lots of hugs and kisses. And help around the house as much as you can.

You will discover a whole lot about love!

And remember,

YOU ARE NOT ALONE.

GLOSSARY (BIG WORDS ABOUT CANCER)

Some of the words you might hear used when someone in your family has cancer.

Benign tumor A growth that is benign does not have cancer, and does not spread to other parts of the body.

Biopsy A biopsy is a test to see if cells have cancer. A small piece of tissue is taken out and looked at under a microscope.

Blood count A sample of blood is taken to examine the number of white cells, red cells, and platelets in the blood.

Bone marrow Bone marrow is the soft, fatty substance that fills the inside cavities of the bones. Blood cells are made in the bone marrow.

Cancer Cancer is a word to describe a large group of diseases (over 100 of them) in which abnormal cells are growing and spreading. Cancer cells are not normal and do not allow room for the normal cells our bodies need.

Cell A cell is the basic structural unit of life. All living things are made up of cells.

Chemotherapy Chemotherapy is the use of drugs to treat cancer.

Detection Discovering the cancer.

Diagnosis The process of identifying a disease by studying its signs and symptoms, making tests, and using existing information to make an accurate decision.

Genes Genes contain hereditary information that is passed from cell to cell as they grow.

IV (Intravenous) Sometimes medicine is put into the bloodstream through the veins. Drugs may drip down from a container through a tube and needle into the vein.

Lymph A clear fluid that travels through the body and contains white blood cells and antibodies.

MRI (Magnetic Resonance Imaging) A test using magnetic fields to produce images of the body.

Malignant tumor A malignant tumor is a big group of cancer cells that may invade other tissues or spread to other parts of the body.

Mammogram A test using low-dose x-rays to produce an image of the breast so the doctor can see if there is a tumor.

Oncology The science dealing with cancer, including its causes and treatments.

Prognosis Prognosis is a prediction what will happen to the disease.

Radiation therapy Radiation is a treatment of cancer with high-energy rays. The rays may be used to shrink the cancer cells or destroy any cells that are left after surgery.

Remission Part or complete disappearance of the cancer as a result of the tests and procedures used to treat it.

Side effects Things that may happen to the cancer patient from the treatments for cancer. Some common side effects are hair loss, sickness, mouth sores, or extreme tiredness.

Surgery An operation to remove cancerous tissue from the body or to find out if cancer is present.

Tumor A tumor is an abnormal swelling or mass of tissue. A tumor can be either benign or malignant.

X-ray A test using radiant energy to diagnose or treat cancer and other diseases.

QUESTIONS TO ASK...

Go ahead and write notes to yourself about questions you want to ask.

Ask my parents: _____

_____

Ask the doctors: _____

_____

Ask my teacher: _____

_____

Ask my church or synagogue leader: _____

_____

Ask others: _____

_____

_____

MY FAMILY IS SPECIAL BECAUSE...

Write some notes to remind yourself what you love about your family.

_____

_____

_____

_____

_____

_____

_____

_____

_____

_____

DRAW YOUR OWN CARTOON ABOUT CANCER!

In this book I've included cartoons about what happened in our family when my mom got cancer.

On this page, you can draw your own cartoon about things that happened when cancer came to your family.

MAKE A LIST OF THE SPECIAL DAYS ON YOUR FAMILY'S CANCER CALENDAR

Date of surgery: _____

Date of first chemotherapy: _____

Date of first radiation treatment: _____

Date of last chemotherapy: _____

Date of last radiation therapy: _____

Other important dates to remember: _____

_____

_____

_____

_____

_____

_____

THE CANCER CLUB

The Cancer Club was formed in 1995 to produce and distribute humorous and helpful products for people with cancer. Its charge is to lift the spirits of those whose lives have been touched by cancer: the patients, family, friends, caregivers, and survivors.

The Cancer Club has a full line of gift items for cancer patients including: books, tapes, custom jewelry, T-shirts, coffee mugs, notepads, etc. A free monthly eNewsletter is published with humorous and uplifting stories about people with cancer.

Christine Clifford, founder and president of The Cancer Club, is available for seminars, workshops and 30–60 minute breakfast, lunch, or dinner speeches. Choose from lectures on health care, motivation, self empowerment, and recovery. Christine addresses conventions, associations, women's events, health care focused events, the corporate arena, and public and private sector organizations.

For more information on The Cancer Club, call or write:

The Cancer Club
PO Box 24747 • Edina MN 55424-0747
(952) 944-0539 • (612) 922-0195 fax
Christine@cancerclub.com · www.cancerclub.com

ABOUT THE AUTHOR

A pioneer in using humor to cope with cancer, Christine Clifford is president and chief executive officer of The Cancer Club, a Minneapolis-based organization that specializes in marketing humorous and helpful products to people with cancer. A cancer survivor herself, and a dynamic public speaker, she currently brings laughter and hope to audiences nationwide with her keynote presentations and seminars about the importance of using humor to cope with chronic disease. Christine is a member of the National Speakers Association.

Christine also is the author of five other books, including *Not Now... I'm Having a No Hair Day: Humor and Healing for People with Cancer, Inspiring Breakthrough Secrets to Live Your Dreams, Cancer Has Its Privileges: Stories of Hope & Laughter, Your Guardian Angel's Gift,* and *YOU, Inc.: The Art of Selling Yourself.* Christine resides in Minneapolis, MN and has lived to see her two boys, Tim and Brooks, graduate from college and become gainfully employed. Don't forget to laugh! ™

ABOUT THE ILLUSTRATOR

Jack Lindstrom specializes in humorous illustration for print. Widely know for his work with William Wells in producing United Feature Syndicate's daily comic strip, "Executive Suite," Lindstrom operates F.A.B. Artists, Inc., an art studio in Minneapolis, Minnesota. Jack is also the illustrator for *Not Now . . . I'm Having a No Hair Day* and *Cancer Has Its Privileges: Stories of Hope and Laughter.*